SECRETS FOR
OF CHRISTM.

The Fragrance
of
CHRISTMAS

CELEBRATION HOPE RELATIONSHIPS INVITATION SHARING TRADITION MUSIC ANTICIPATION SAVIOUR
SECRETS FOR A SEASON OF C. H. R. I. S. T. M. A. S. SPIRIT

SECRETS FOR A SEASON
OF CHRISTMAS SPIRIT

The Fragrance of CHRISTMAS

DAN & DAVE DAVIDSON
WITH BECCA LYNN

NEW LEAF PRESS

First printing: September 1998
Fifth printing: September 2005

ISBN: 0-89221-425-2
Library of Congress Number: 98-66304

Unless otherwise noted, Bible Scripture is from the New International Version.

Cover design by Janell Robertson
Interior design by Brent Spurlock and Janell Robertson
Essays are a collaboration between Dan and Dave Davidson

Printed in the United States of America.

Please visit our website for other great titles: www.newleafpress.net

For information regarding publicity for author
interviews, contact the publicity department at (870) 438-5288.

Presented to:

_____

Presented by:

_____

Date:

_____

The Fragrance of Christmas

*Y*ou can see it, you can hear it, the secrets of the Christmas spirit. Our senses seize the seasonal surroundings of scotch pine and spiced apples as the incense of hot punch mixes with a wreath's evergreen branches. While sipping hot tea or eggnog, cinnamon candles blend in with Grandma's cooking. The aroma of burning cedar wafts into the room as the sweet smells reveal secrets of Christmas past, present, and future.

While holiday traditions spark a rekindling inside the heart, seasonal preparations and expectations are embraced as decorations are set in place. Hospitality of the heart and home encourage times of reflection as angels point us to a place where God gives eternal peace and grace.

Attempting to capture the feeling and fragrance of Christmas is an original acronym for C.H.R.I.S.T.M.A.S. . . . Celebration, Hope, Relationships, Invitation, Sharing, Tradition, Music, Anticipation, Saviour.

It is our prayer that you will experience the full Fragrance of Christmas — while sharing with friends and family these secrets of the Christmas spirit.

Dan & Dave Davidson

THANKS BE TO GOD, WHO ALWAYS
LEADS US IN TRIUMPHAL PROCESSION
IN CHRIST AND THROUGH US SPREADS
EVERYWHERE THE FRAGRANCE OF THE
KNOWLEDGE OF HIM.
2 CORINTHIANS 2:14

CELEBRATION SHOULD START
FROM WITHIN THE HEART.

CELEBRATION

SUDDENLY A GREAT COMPANY OF THE HEAVENLY HOST
APPEARED WITH THE ANGEL, PRAISING GOD AND SAYING,
"GLORY TO GOD IN THE HIGHEST, AND ON EARTH PEACE TO MEN
ON WHOM HIS FAVOR RESTS."

LUKE 2:13-14

CELEBRATION HOPE RELATIONSHIPS INVITATION SHARING TRADITION MUSIC ANTICIPATION SAVIOUR
SECRETS FOR A SEASON OF C. H. R. I. S. T. M. A. S. SPIRIT

The Fragrance of Christmas

Christmas is a joyous time of celebration. We all may celebrate in different ways: a neighborhood gathering of friends, a family Christmas dinner, a Sunday school church pageant, a concert of cold-nosed carolers, a moonlit walk on new fallen snow, a quiet time of devotion or reflection by a warm winter fire.

Whereas the true celebration of the Christmas spirit often takes place during the festivities of the season — at any time of the year we can choose to celebrate the miracle of the manger within each of our hearts.

WHOSE BIRTHDAY ARE YOU CELEBRATING?

THEY WILL CELEBRATE YOUR ABUNDANT GOODNESS
AND JOYFULLY SING OF YOUR RIGHTEOUSNESS.
PSALM 145:7

Children look forward to birthday parties with great excitement every year. The friends, the gifts, the cake, the balloons, the games — it's a time of celebration.

Four-year-old Matt had heard from his family that Christmas was Jesus' birthday. On Christmas morning after everyone had opened presents, he asked about the "rest of Christmas."

His mother reminded him of all the gifts he had received. Matt then said with a perplexed look, "Christmas can't be over, where's the cake and candles — we haven't had a birthday party for Jesus."

In his heart, he had wondered why his family hadn't given Jesus a birthday party. Why did everyone else get presents instead of Jesus?

"Isn't Jesus sad because we forgot to celebrate His birthday?" questioned Matt.

Realizing that Matt had truly begun to understand the true spirit of Christmas, his mom did some quick thinking and said, "We can still have a party for Jesus. I'll invite some of your friends and neighbors over later today. I'll bake a cake, and we will celebrate His birthday!"

The Christmas season is filled with singing, gifts, decorations, and parties. Joy is shared among friends and family. The question that young Matt brings to our heart is — whose birthday will you be celebrating this year at Christmas?

HOLIDAY CELEBRATIONS SPARK JOY AND BRING
AN AIR OF FAMILIAR HAPPINESS TO ALL AROUND.
Becca Lynn

We decorated six trees each Christmas: a large one for the
living room and five small ones for each child's room. The children
would each have to create their decorations and put them on the trees.
We all gathered in the living room to decorate the big tree together.
I inspected all the trees and awarded prizes for the most beautiful,
most original, most colorful, most heartwarming, and most
unusual, etc. As you can guess, everyone got a prize.

Art Linkletter

COME CHRISTMAS EVE, THE ANDERSON FAMILY WOULD GATHER
AT TWILIGHT-TIME. THE CHILDREN DRESSED IN SEASONAL GALA GARB,
THE ADULTS IN SUNDAY BEST. SWEDISH JOY AND THE AROMATIC SCENT OF CARDAMOM
ROLLS FILLED EACH AND EVERY ROOM OF THE CANDLELIT HOME. GRANDMA AND
GRANDPA GREETED VISITORS WITH HEARTY HUGS AND KISSES,
SCURRYING THEM IN FROM THE BLISTERING COLD.

Becca Lynn

GOD BLESS US EVERY ONE

At last the dinner was all done, the cloth was cleared, the hearth swept, and the fire made up. The compound in the jug being tasted, and considered perfect, apples and oranges were put upon the table, and a shovel-full of chestnuts on the fire. Then all the Cratchit family drew round the hearth, in what Bob Cratchit called a circle, meaning half a one; and at Bob Cratchit's elbow stood the family display of glass. Two tumblers, and a custard-cup without a handle.

These held the hot stuff from the jug, however, as well as golden goblets would have done; and Bob served it out with beaming looks, while the chestnuts on the fire sputtered and cracked noisily. Then Bob proposed: "A Merry Christmas to us all, my dears. God bless us!"

Which all the family re-echoed. "God bless us every one!"

From *A Christmas Carol* by Charles Dickens, 1812-1870

CHRISTMAS BISCUITS

Delicious English biscuits for any festive season.

Ingredients:
1 cup all-purpose flour
2 teaspoons allspice
1 teaspoon ground cinnamon
1/4 cup butter or margarine
1/4 cup brown sugar
1 egg

Preheat oven to 400° degrees. Grease cookie sheets. In a large bowl, sift together the flour, allspice, and cinnamon. Cut in the butter or margarine and mix with a fork. Stir in the sugar and add the egg, mixing to a stiff dough.

Knead dough on a floured surface until smooth. Roll out dough thinly. Cut into various shapes with cookie cutters. Place on cookie sheets and bake for 12 minutes or until golden. Let cool in the pan for a few minutes, then transfer to a wire rack. Store in an airtight container. Makes 14 cookies.

A PARTY FOR THE PRINCE OF PEACE

Have a party in honor of Him whose birth we celebrate. Include in the celebration an older person who would otherwise be alone, someone you have just met, a young person away from home, and one or two very special friends such as a pastor or teacher who is important to your family's life.

Some special things to make or do might include birthday card place cards — a special star-shaped cake with white and yellow icing full of fruit to represent the fulfillment of the seed of promise. A table centerpiece of a basket or small wooden box of clean straw surrounded by small packages made to represent gold, frankincense, and myrrh. Someone might tell about the three gifts and what they might have represented or how they might have been used.

Gloria Gaither & Shirley Dobson

A FRAGRANT PRAYER
FATHER, MY HEART REJOICES JUST AS THE ANGELS
DID FOR YOUR MIRACLE IN THE MANGER.
BECAUSE OF YOUR GRACE I CAN JOYFULLY CELEBRATE THE
GLORIOUS BIRTH AND RESURRECTION OF JESUS.
NO WONDER WISE MEN STILL FOLLOW YOU, LORD.

HOPE IS RESTORED
IN JESUS OUR LORD.

MAY THE GOD OF HOPE FILL YOU WITH ALL JOY AND PEACE
AS YOU TRUST IN HIM, SO THAT YOU MAY OVERFLOW WITH
HOPE BY THE POWER OF THE HOLY SPIRIT.
ROMANS 15:13

CELEBRATION HOPE RELATIONSHIPS INVITATION SHARING TRADITION MUSIC ANTICIPATION SAVIUOR
SECRETS FOR A SEASON OF C. H. R. I. S. T. M. A. S. SPIRIT

The Fragrance of Christmas

Christmas is a merry time for most but a sad season for many. Those who are alone, under hardship, or who are ill may find it hard to grasp the Christmas spirit. Thankfully, the miracle of the Christ child born in Bethlehem is what still gives genuine hope to all those who are hurting today.

No matter what our circumstances in life, God is ready to offer His hope of restoration and renewal to anyone willing to receive Him this Christmas season.

WE NEED CHRISTMAS
TO WAKE US UP,
TO BRING US BACK,
TO JOG OUR MEMORIES,
TO REMIND US AGAIN
OF WHAT THIS LIFE IS ALL ABOUT.
James W. Moore

TASTE AND SEE THAT THE LORD IS GOOD

BUT AS FOR ME, I WILL ALWAYS HAVE HOPE;
I WILL PRAISE YOU MORE AND MORE.
PSALM 71:14

Imagine a toddler enjoying a candy cane at Christmas. With each lick of the holiday treat, the child's happiness seems to provide insulation from the burdens of the busy season. God plants hope for the future in the innocent and joyful hearts of children.

Perhaps the Psalmist had this in mind when he wrote in Psalm 34:8, *Taste and see that the Lord is good. . . .*

Did you know that the candy cane illustrates the Christmas story of God's love for us through His Son? This legend can help us share the message of the manger with others.

It all began with an Indiana candymaker's inspiration to create a candy reflecting the true meaning of Christmas and the attributes of Jesus' life. Pure white candy became the symbolization for the miraculous virgin birth and perfect nature of Jesus. The hard candy stick reflected Christ as the *Solid Rock* (Psalm 62:1-2) in which we trust, built on the foundation and stability of God's faithfulness.

The clever "J" shape reminds us of the wonderful name of Jesus and depicts the staff of the "Good Shepherd" who is willing to go out of His way to rescue His lost sheep who have strayed.

The candymaker then incorporated red stripes for the redeeming blood shed when Jesus was scourged before being nailed to the cross. The stripes of Jesus, which heal us from sin, were prophesied in Isaiah 53, long before His birth in Bethlehem.

The next time you taste a candy cane, remember this illustration of hope through Christ's perfect love for us. This Christmas season, with childlike joy and faith, take time to "taste and see that the Lord is good."

ONCE EACH YEAR, CHRISTMAS COMES ALONG TO RENEW
OUR HOPE AND TO REMIND US THAT THE DARKNESS OF THIS WORLD
CANNOT OVERCOME THE LIGHT OF THE LORD.
James W. Moore

CHRISTMAS HOPE IN GOD

The past Christmas had been lean. The children's gifts had come from cereal coupons, mail-in offers for free items, second-hand thrift stores, and Toys for Tots.

This year was even leaner. Some would call it bleak. I knew God was in control. My peace of mind was from His grace. If there was nothing under the tree besides dried-up pine needles, I knew God would have His purposes for that.

A week before Christmas, my insurance agent knocked on the front door, walked in, and handed me a thousand dollars cash from his immediate and extended families. It was the kind of thing that no one but God could have accomplished. We were overwhelmed. My hope had not been in God giving us money. My hope had been in God's sovereignty and care.

Much hope in thin ice will get you an icy bath. Little hope in thick ice will still allow you to skate. The amount of hope is not the deciding factor. The object of the hope is that God's character stands behind His promise of care for us. He cannot lie. He keeps His every promise.

I have no guarantee of how He will keep His promise, only that His choice will be for His greatest glory and my greatest good.

Tim Moser

If I could have a special dream
Coming true on Christmas morn;
I would want the world to see how
His Father smiled when Christ was born.
The greatest gift the world has known. . . .

Amy Grant from "Love Has Come"

HE BROUGHT PEACE ON EARTH
AND WANTS TO BRING IT ALSO
INTO YOUR SOUL — THAT PEACE WHICH
THE WORLD CANNOT GIVE. HE IS THE ONE WHO
WOULD SAVE HIS PEOPLE FROM THEIR SINS.

Corrie Ten Boom

CHRISTMAS WREATHS

by: Ingrid from CookieRecipe.com

Easy to fix, attractive, and tasty.

Ingredients:
1 1/4 cups butter or margarine
3/4 cup confectioner's sugar
2 1/2 cups all-purpose flour
3/4 teaspoon peppermint extract
red food coloring
green food coloring

1. Preheat oven to 375° degrees.
2. Cream together the butter or margarine, confectioner's sugar, flour, and peppermint extract. Mix well.
3. Separate dough into two equal parts, put into separate bowls, and tint with food-coloring. Roll dough into small balls, approximately 1/2 tsp. per cookie. Place six balls in a circle, alternating colors onto cookie sheet.
4. Bake for 8 minutes. Makes 3 dozen.

A CHILD WHO FOUND GOD

*T*he children were helping decorate the house for Christmas. As they set up the nativity set, they discovered the baby Jesus was missing. Imagine a nativity set with no baby Jesus!

Suddenly, two-year-old Clinton popped up from behind the davenport, holding high the missing Babe and excitedly called, "Look, I found God!"

May we all be able to say the same!

Venus E. Bardanouve

A FRAGRANT PRAYER

YOU RICHLY BLESS ALL WHO CALL ON YOU . . . EVERYONE
DOING SO WILL BE SAVED. FATHER, THIS IS THE HOPE
OF YOUR WORD. ITS TRUTH IS BASED ON YOU! YOU
CANNOT LIE. YOUR PROMISES ENDURE FOREVER.
THANK YOU FOR THE GIFT OF LIVING HOPE.

RELATIONSHIPS ARE RENEWED
BY GRACE AND GRATITUDE.

*R*ELATIONSHIPS

MAY THE LORD MAKE YOUR LOVE INCREASE

AND OVERFLOW FOR EACH OTHER AND FOR EVERYONE ELSE.

1 Thessalonians 3:12

CELEBRATION HOPE RELATIONSHIPS INVITATION SHARING TRADITION MUSIC ANTICIPATION SAVIOUR
SECRETS FOR A SEASON OF C. H. R. I. S. T. M. A. S. SPIRIT

The Fragrance of Christmas

*C*enturies ago mistletoe was considered a symbol of peace. Soldiers made a temporary truce and discarded their weapons when under mistletoe. In ancient Briton, it was hung in doorways to ward evil away. Visitors were often offered a warm welcome kiss after a safe entrance.

THE FRAGRANCE OF CHRISTMAS IS FOUND . . .
KISSING THE ONE YOU LOVE SO UNDERNEATH THE MISTLETOE.

Dan and Dave Davidson

THE GIFT OF TIME

*Therefore encourage one another and build
each other up, just as in fact you are doing.*
1 Thessalonians 5:11

*I*t's been said that money can't buy happiness. In the same manner, material gifts can't take the place of time and love shared in close relationships with others.

Whether it be drawing nearer to neighbors, deepening romantic love with your sweetheart, or strengthening family ties, the gift of time shows your commitment of love and friendship like nothing else can.

James Moore illustrates this point in his book, *Christmas Gifts That Always Fit* with the following story: "The greatest gift I ever received," said a respected and successful attorney, "was a gift I got one Christmas when my dad gave me a small box. Inside was a note: *'Son, this year I will give you 365 hours, an hour a day, every day after dinner. It's yours! We'll talk about what you want to talk about. We'll go where you want to go or we'll play what you want to play. It will be your hour! This is my gift to you this year; the gift of time!'*"

My dad not only kept his promise, but that time together became so special to us that he renewed it every year. It's the greatest Christmas gift I ever received."

This Christmas consider giving the gift of time and love to a special loved one. It just may be the most profound and enduring gift of a lifetime.

INTERPERSONAL RELATIONSHIPS ARE
THE MOST VALUED AND CHERISHED GIFTS OF ALL.
THE BIBLE TEACHES THAT GOD GAVE A PERSON
AS A GIFT TO EVERY ONE OF US, AND THAT PERSON
IS JESUS CHRIST.
Billy Graham

HAPPY, HAPPY CHRISTMAS

*C*hristmas family party! We know nothing in nature more delightful! There seems a magic in the very name of Christmas. Petty jealousies and discords are forgotten. Social feelings are awakened — father and son, or brother and sister, who have met and passed with averted gaze, or a look of cold recognition for months before, proffer and return the cordial embrace and bury their past animosities in their present happiness.

Kindly hearts that have yearned toward each other, but have been withheld by false notions of pride and self-dignity, are again reunited and all is kindness and benevolence! Would that Christmas lasted the whole year through (as it ought) and that the prejudices and passions which deform our better nature were never called into action among those to whom they should ever be strangers!

From *Sketches by Boz* by Charles Dickens, 1812-1870

"DEAR LORD JESUS, BE OUR GUEST, AND MAY THIS FOOD TO US BE BLESSED. AMEN."
SWEDISH SAUSAGE, LINGONBERRIES, AND RICE PUDDING WERE PRESENTED TO THE CHILDREN
IN THE KITCHEN, ADULTS IN THE FORMAL LIVING ROOM. LAUGHTER AND LOVE GLOWED
BRIGHTER THIS NIGHT THAN ALL OTHERS IN THE YEAR COMBINED.

Becca Lynn

WHO IS MOVING AT CHRISTMAS?

There's an old story about an elderly couple. They had the radio on one day as they drove through the busy streets, and as they listened to the beautiful music of Christmas, the wife became nostalgic: "Herbert, do you remember when we were younger, we used to sit so close together as we drove along? It was so wonderful back then. What happened?"

"I don't know about that," said Herbert. "All I know is . . . I haven't moved."

Christmas comes each year to remind us that God is not the one who has moved away from us. We are the ones who have moved. We are the ones who have drifted away from Him.

James Moore

A FRAGRANT PRAYER

THANK YOU FOR THE GIFT OF FRIENDS AND FAMILY.
PEOPLE IN MY LIFE ARE AN IMPORTANT PART OF MY FAITH.
HELP ME TO LOVE OTHERS AS YOU HAVE COMMANDED.
THANK YOU, FATHER, FOR REVEALING YOURSELF IN
THE RELATIONSHIPS YOU HAVE BLESSED ME WITH.

AN INVITATION EXTENDS
LOVE TO FAMILY AND FRIENDS.

INVITATION

SHARE WITH GOD'S PEOPLE WHO
ARE IN NEED. PRACTICE HOSPITALITY.
Romans 12:13

CELEBRATION HOPE RELATIONSHIPS INVITATION SHARING TRADITION MUSIC ANTICIPATION SAVIOUR
SECRETS FOR A SEASON OF C. H. R. I. S. T. M. A. S. SPIRIT

The Fragrance of Christmas

*S*imple words of encouragement, a gift of reassurance, an act of compassion — these are all blessings that can be attached to an invitation. There are many ways we can reach out to others during Christmas. When we invite family and friends into our homes and our hearts, we let them know how special and loved they are.

Christmas itself is an invitation from God. He invites everyone to the manger to experience the perfect love of the Christ Child offered as a sacrifice for all.

An Invitation from Heaven

*M*ost of us open our homes to others at Christmas with graciousness and hospitality. Ralph Waldo Emerson once said, "The ornament of a house is the friends who frequent it."

A warm welcome message is usually our intention, but because of the busyness of the season, we may be sending out confusing signals to those we care about.

Patsy Clairmont speaks of the year her family planned to write "NOEL" in lights on their house. They got a late start and finished only half the project because of bad weather. That left a multi-colored "NO" flashing on her rooftop. She said they had fewer guests that year.

Has the holiday rush and stress of the season caused your family to say "NO" to friends, family, and neighbors? Even more importantly, have you invited the Lord into your celebration of Christmas, or have you said "NO" to Him, also?

There is a cave in the Church of the Nativity in Bethlehem which many believe to be the actual birthplace of Christ. As William Barclay writes, "There is something beautiful in the symbolism that the church where the cave is had a door so low that all must stoop to enter. It is supremely fitting that every man should approach the infant Jesus upon his knees."

God's message is always clear. He says "YES" to all who believe. At Christmas He invites us to come to the cave and humble our hearts toward heaven.

IF HE HAD KNOWN WHO WERE THE GUESTS THAT STARRY NIGHT,

THE INNKEEPER WOULD HAVE EAGERLY OFFERED

HIS OWN BED, THE BEST HE HAD.

Sarah Hornsby

A Family Welcome Wreath

*T*ake a green wreath and decorate it with whatever characterizes the special memories and interests of each family member during the past year: a Scout badge, a small ballet shoe, a memento from a campout trip, a tiny bride and groom to recall a family wedding.

With florist wire and picks, attach these items to the wreath, and weave bright thin ribbon in and out in a festive way. It is simplest to buy the wreath and make it your own with your mementos, ribbons, and decorations.

Hang the wreath on your front door to welcome all who come in during the holiday season. Then after Christmas, cover the wreath with a big clear plastic sack, and save it as a "snapshot of your year — a little bit of history."

Cheri Fuller

THE ONLY BLIND PERSON AT CHRISTMAS-TIME
IS HE WHO HAS NOT CHRISTMAS IN HIS HEART.

Helen Keller

An Innkeeper with a Heart

Wally was nine that Christmas and in the second grade. He was big and clumsy, slow in movement and mind, but was still well-liked by the other children in his class.

He was selected to be the innkeeper in the annual Christmas pageant. After Joseph had pleaded for a place to rest, Wally was prompted to say his line, "No, be gone!"

Joseph placed his arm around Mary as she laid her head upon her husband's shoulder and the two of them started to move away. The innkeeper did not return inside the inn, however. Wally stood there in the doorway, watching the forlorn couple. His mouth was open, his brow creased with concern, his eyes filling unmistakably with tears.

And suddenly this Christmas pageant became different from all others.

"Don't go Joseph," Wally called out. "Bring Mary back." Wallace Purling's face grew into a bright smile. "You can have my room."

Adapted from Dina Donohue

CHRISTMAS CARD PRAYER LINK

*U*se Christmas cards as a link to real people and their needs through the Christmas season and the month of January. Choose one Christmas card each day from those received.

Read the whole card aloud and pass it around the family circle. Do this at a regular time like bedtime or after supper or at breakfast time.

Have special prayer together for each person in the family that sent the card. Send a postcard to that family to tell them about your Christmas card prayers and that their card was the one chosen on this day.

They will appreciate knowing that your family prayed today for their family.

Gloria Gaither & Shirley Dobson

THE HOUR IS SWEPT AND GARNISHED; THE WALK HAS BEEN
BRUSHED, AND THE STAIR; THE CRYSTAL AND SILVER ARE GLEAMING
BUT OH, IS THE CHRIST CHILD THERE?

Lela Bassford

THE FRAGRANCE OF CHRISTMAS IS FOUND . . .
MAKING ANGELS IN THE SNOW;
WARMING UP WITH HOT COCOA.

Dan and Dave Davidson

Few things in life compare to lying on one's back while making a snow
angel in freshly fallen ivory powder, with the night sky overhead flaunting
her grandeur. A shooting star falls and there is a rush inside, for it will
never occur again, and you were witness to a winter splendor.
How much better to share this twinkling moment, reaching out
to hold a hand, words not expected, words not needed.

Becca Lynn

A FRAGRANT PRAYER
THANK YOU FOR YOUR INVITATION TO BETHLEHEM.
YOUR LOVE ENABLES ME TO OPEN MY HEART TO OTHERS.
I AM SO GRATEFUL THAT IT IS YOUR DESIRE THAT EVERYONE
WOULD COME TO KNOW THE CHRIST CHILD IN A STABLE.
HELP ME TO INVITE OTHERS INTO YOUR KINGDOM.

SHARING LOVE AS A GIFT
WILL INSPIRE AND UPLIFT.

*S*HARING

AND DO NOT FORGET TO DO GOOD AND SHARE
WITH OTHERS, FOR WITH SUCH SACRIFICES GOD IS PLEASED.

Hebrews 13:16

CELEBRATION HOPE RELATIONSHIPS INVITATION SHARING TRADITION MUSIC ANTICIPATION SAVIOUR
SECRETS FOR A SEASON OF C. H. R. I. S. T. M. A. S. SPIRIT

The Fragrance of Christmas

Christmas is known by all as a season of gift-giving. Sharing gifts has become a tradition that allows us to show others we really do care. In addition to presents under the tree, there are other gifts of compassion, kindness, charity, and forgiveness, which can only come from the heart.

God's heart has given us the greatest gift of all. Beginning on that starry night when shepherds heard the angels sing, He shared His life with us.

THE BLESSING OF GIVING FROM THE HEART

IT IS MORE BLESSED TO GIVE THAN TO RECEIVE.
Acts 20:35

The true spirit of giving can be found in the loving hearts of children. The following story illustrates an innocent and unconditional love a daughter expressed to her father, which became a lifelong inspiration for him.

After a 3-year-old girl decorated a box and put it under the family Christmas tree, her father scolded her for wasting a roll of expensive gold wrapping paper.

Nevertheless, she still brought the gift to him the next morning and said, "This is for you Daddy." When he opened it and found that the box was empty, his anger flared again.

"Don't you know that when you give someone a present, there's supposed to be something inside of it?" yelled the father.

The little girl looked up at him with tears in her eyes and said, "Oh Daddy, it's not empty. I blew kisses into the box. All for you, Daddy."

The father was crushed. He put his arms around his little girl, and begged her forgiveness. He kept the gold box by his bed for years. Whenever he was discouraged, he would take out an imaginary kiss and remember the love his daughter shared that Christmas morning.

God's Word tells us that it is truly more blessed to give than receive. This principle is one that is reflected year after year during the Christmas season. When sharing a gift with someone, we've often heard that *it's the thought that counts.* This story reminds us that it's also the *love* that counts.

IF WE THINK OF OUR HEART, RATHER THAN OUR PURSE, AS THE RESERVOIR
OF OUR GIVING, WE SHALL FIND IT FULL ALL THE TIME!
David Dunn

THE FRAGRANCE OF CHRISTMAS IS FOUND . . .
SHARING HOLIDAY REGARDS
IN CHRISTMAS CARDS.

Dan and Dave Davidson

The first Christmas card was sent in 1843 in England. It was
popularized in America by Louis Prang, a German printer whose
cards depicted family Christmas and nativity scenes.

Somehow not only for Christmas
But all the long year through,
The joy that you give to others
Is the joy that comes back to you.
And the more you spend in blessing
The poor and lonely and sad
The more of your heart's possessing
Returns to make you glad.
John Greenleaf Whittier

43

Family Food Basket

*P*ut a small basket in the center of your dining room table and encourage each person, big and small, to do little odd jobs and earn extra money to put in the basket.

Each family member contributes something, no matter how small. Then, just before Christmas, parents and children go to the grocery store to select items for a holiday food basket for a less fortunate family in the community.

God is the greatest giver at Christmastime.
It's impossible for anyone to out-give Him.

Dave Davidson

The tree in the front window dazzled in silver tinsel.
It is in this sentimental shade of the holidays,
the aroma of old-fashioned cooking, and in the gift-
giving memories held dear, all the peaceful love of
Christmas is reflected and remembered in
the eyes of a five year old.

Becca Lynn

THE MAGI, AS YOU KNOW,
WERE WISE MEN —
WONDERFULLY WISE MEN —
WHO BROUGHT GIFTS TO THE BABE
IN THE MANGER.
THEY INVENTED THE ART
OF GIVING CHRISTMAS PRESENTS.

O Henry

When the song of the angels is still —
when the star in the sky is gone —
when the kings and princes are back home —
when the shepherds have returned to their flocks,
the work of Christmas begins. . . .

To find the lost, to heal the broken,
to feed the hungry, to release the prisoners,
to rebuild the nations, to bring peace among people,
to take music in the heart. Or, in other words,
to do the work of Christ.

Howard Thurman

A FRAGRANT PRAYER

LORD, YOU HAVE TAUGHT ME TO SHARE MY FAITH.
USE ME TO BLESS OTHERS THIS CHRISTMAS SEASON.
MAY THE CARDS, GIFTS, SMILES, AND PRAYERS I
SHARE BE A REFLECTION OF YOUR HOLY SPIRIT.
HUMBLE ME, LORD, THAT I MAY GLORIFY YOU.

TRADITION IS A KEY
FOR A FAMILY LEGACY.

YOUR STATUTES ARE MY HERITAGE FOREVER;
THEY ARE THE JOY OF MY HEART.

Psalm 119:111

CELEBRATION HOPE RELATIONSHIPS INVITATION SHARING TRADITION MUSIC ANTICIPATION SAVIOUR
SECRETS FOR A SEASON OF C. H. R. I. S. T. M. A. S. SPIRIT

The Fragrance of Christmas

There are few traditions stronger than those built through the years around our celebration of Christmas. The customs handed down from a family tree, the heritage drawn from various cultures, and the traditions we ourselves have originated — all create a foundational family legacy that will continue to inspire for generations to come.

God uses His heritage of hope to demonstrate His love for us, built on the Solid Rock of His Son. His promise of love will never change — for He is the same, yesterday, today, and tomorrow.

TREASURED TRADITIONS OF THE SEASON

THEN, OPENING THEIR TREASURE CHESTS, THEY OFFERED
HIM GIFTS OF GOLD, FRANKINCENSE AND MYRRH.
Matthew 2:11

*T*he tradition of gift-giving is rooted in the Magi's act of bearing gifts to the infant Jesus and in the realization that Christ was a gift from God to the world.

In England, Victorians exchanged gifts on New Year's Day until the late 1800s when the custom shifted to Christmas Day. The thought and creativity behind the giving became far more important than the gift itself. This story by Gerald Horton Bath illustrates the Christmas tradition of giving.

The African boy listened carefully as the teacher explained why it is that Christians give presents to each other on Christmas Day. "The gift is an expression of our joy over the birth of Jesus and our friendship for each other," she said.

When Christmas Day came, the boy brought to the teacher a seashell of lustrous beauty. "Where did you ever find such a beautiful shell?" the teacher asked as she gently fingered the gift.

The youth told her that there was only one spot where such extraordinary shells could be found. When he named the place, a certain bay several miles away, the teacher was left speechless.

"Why . . . why, it's gorgeous . . . wonderful, but you shouldn't have gone all that way to get a gift for me."

His eyes brightening, the boy answered, "Long walk part of gift."

Treasured traditions shared with others can be a tremendous blessing at Christmas. Time is measured, lessons are learned, and memories are made by cherished family customs centered on the celebration of Jesus' birth.

ARE YOU WILLING TO BELIEVE THAT LOVE
IS THE STRONGEST THING IN THE WORLD?
IF SO, THEN YOU CAN KEEP CHRISTMAS.
AND, IF YOU KEEP IT FOR A DAY, WHY NOT ALWAYS?
Henry Van Dyke

THE FRAGRANCE OF CHRISTMAS IS FOUND . . .
DAD'S GOING ALL OUT
SHOVELING A SNOW ROUTE.
Dan and Dave Davidson

FATHER'S EYES SPARKLED AT CHRISTMAS TIME. BY LATE DECEMBER THE WATER IN THE BACKYARD POND WAS FROZEN AND DAD MARVELED IN THE POTENTIAL OF A SKATING SEASON. AS SOON AS MY BROTHER AND I SHOWED INTEREST IN WOBBLING AROUND ON COLD STEEL, DAD USED AN OLD SNOW-BLOWER TO CREATE ICE MAZES, PINWHEEL PATHS AND HOCKEY RINKS. HE CLEARED THE GARAGE AND SET UP LONG WOODEN BENCHES WHERE THE NEIGHBORHOOD CHILDREN LACED UP THEIR SKATES. INSIDE, MOM HEATED UP COCOA AND STOKED A FIRE IN THE LARGE STONE FIREPLACE. NEIGHBORHOOD CHILDREN GATHERED TO SHARE MY FATHER'S SNOW PATHS. I REMEMBER MY IMMENSE PRIDE AND THE SEASONAL UNITY CREATED JUST BECAUSE ONE MAN CARED. **THANKS, DAD**.

Becca Lynn

Family traditions are the threads that
link one generation to the next.
Richard Exley

HOME FOR CHRISTMAS

*T*his is meeting time again. Home is the magnet. The winter land roars and hums with the eager speed of return journeys.

The dark is noisy and bright with late-night arrivals — doors thrown open, running shadows on snow, open arms, kisses, voices, and laughter, laughter at everything and nothing. Inarticulate, giddy, and confused are those original minutes of being back again.

The very familiarity of everything acts like shock. Contentment has to be drawn in slowly, steadyingly, in deep breaths — there is so much of it. We rely on home not to change, and it does not, wherefore we give thanks. Again Christmas: abiding point of return. Set apart by its mystery, mood, and magic, the season seems in a way to stand outside time.

All that is dear, that is lasting, renews its hold on us; we are home again.

Elizabeth Bowen

MY PARENTS ALWAYS MADE CHRISTMAS A GIVING TIME — OF THEMSELVES. . . .
THE WARM CINNAMONY SMELL FROM MAMA'S KITCHEN, THE HUM OF HER SEWING MACHINE
AND THE CRISP CEDAR CURLS IN DADDY'S WORKSHOP SPOKE OF CARING.
Sarah Hornsby

Caramel Fondue

GREAT FOR DIPPING SLICED APPLES

1/2 cup butter
2 cups brown sugar
1 cup light corn syrup
1 cup sweetened condensed milk
1 tsp. vanilla

Melt butter, add sugar and syrup
Bring to boil and stir in milk
Boil and stir to soft ball stage
(using candy thermometer)
Remove from heat and add vanilla

Will keep in refrigerator for up to two months.
Heat and serve with sliced apples for dipping.

THE FRAGRANCE OF CHRISTMAS IS FOUND . . .
A BAH-HUMBUG
SWEPT UNDER THE RUG.
Dan and Dave Davidson

The Grinch stole Christmas,
but in the end gave it back.
Scrooge said "Bah-Humbug,"
but later caught the Christmas spirit.
Embrace the traditions that make up
your family's Christmas legacy.

Dave Davidson

A FRAGRANT PRAYER
ETERNAL FATHER, THANK YOU FOR PRESERVING THE
CHRISTMAS STORY IN YOUR HOLY WORD. HELP ME PASS
YOUR MESSAGE OF LOVE AND PEACE ON TO TO MY CHILDREN
SO THAT THEIR HEARTS WILL KNOW YOUR SAVING GRACE.
THANKS FOR YOUR HERITAGE OF HOPE FOR MY FAMILY.

MUSIC IS THE EMOTION
OF WORSHIP AND DEVOTION.

AND AGAIN, WHEN GOD BRINGS HIS FIRSTBORN INTO THE WORLD,
HE SAYS, "LET ALL GOD'S ANGELS WORSHIP HIM."
Hebrews 1:6

CELEBRATION HOPE RELATIONSHIPS INVITATION SHARING TRADITION MUSIC ANTICIPATION SAVIOUR
SECRETS FOR A SEASON OF C. H. R. I. S. T. M. A. S. SPIRIT

The Fragrance of Christmas

Music can capture the Christmas spirit like nothing else in life. Whether it be the simple faith expressed in a children's pageant chorus, the joy shared among merry carolers, or the worshipful grandeur of Handel's "Messiah" — music becomes the emotional heartbeat of Christmas worship and devotion.

God sent His angels to sing and proclaim the glorious news of His Son's birth on that first Christmas night. The same Good News can be music to our soul even today if we will only listen.

SOUNDS OF THE SEASON

SING TO HIM A NEW SONG;
PLAY SKILLFULLY, AND SHOUT FOR JOY.
Psalm 33:3

*S*ometimes when things go wrong, opportunities are created for inspiration and blessing. It was an assistant pastor and organist who responded to some holiday stress, and collaborated to write the most popular Christmas carol in the world.

On Christmas Eve in 1818, the priests in St. Nicolas Church, Obendorf, Austria, panicked when the church organ broke down. The assistant pastor quickly wrote a six-stanza poem beginning with "Stille nacht, heilige nacht." Franz Gruber, the church organist, then arranged a melody for two solo voices, a chorus, and guitar to be sung that same night.

An organ repairman learned of the song and happened to take a copy home with him. Two traveling singing families later sang it for the king of Prussia and in New York City. In 1834 the classic carol was heard in English, "Silent Night, Holy Night."

God used a broken organ, three godly men, and a guitar to illustrate the Christmas story in a simple yet profound musical message. For over 150 years this carol has touched the hearts of millions, reflecting God's love through the birth of His Son.

Your Christmas celebrations may not always turn out just as you plan, either. But, there are no coincidences in the eyes of God. He may be preparing you for a new plan.

As you celebrate the season in song this year, remember that God works everything together for good for those that love Him. Be ready for God to bless you in His way this holiday season.

I DO HOPE YOUR CHRISTMAS HAS HAD A LITTLE TOUCH OF ETERNITY

IN AMONG THE RUSH AND PITTER PATTER AND ALL.

Evelyn Underhill

A NEW TWIST ON A CAROL

*O*ne Sunday evening, I overheard my five year old, Julie, practicing *"Hark the Herald Angels Sing,"* a song she'd been rehearsing that morning in church for next week's Christmas program.

It was all I could do to suppress my laughter when, in place of "which angelic hosts proclaim," Julie sang, "with the jelly toast proclaim."

Marilyn Clark

WHETHER IT BE CAROLERS AT YOUR DOOR, HOLIDAY HARPISTS,
CHURCH HAND BELL CHOIRS, OR YOUR CHILD'S PRESCHOOL PROGRAM,
MUSIC WARMS THE HEARTS OF YOUNG AND OLD AT CHRISTMAS.

Becca Lynn

CAROLS IN THE COTSWOLDS

*C*rossing, at last, the frozen millstream . . . we climbed up to Joseph's farm. We grouped ourselves round the farmhouse porch. The sky cleared, and broad streams of stars ran down over the valley . . . we started singing, and we were all moved by the words and the sudden trueness of our voices. Pure, very clear, and breathless we sang:

> *As Joseph was a-walking, he heard an angel sing,*
> *"This night shall be the birth-time of Christ the Heavenly King."*

And two thousand Christmases became real to us then; the houses, the halls, the places of paradise had all been visited; the stars were bright to guide the kings through the snow; and across the farmyard we could hear the beasts in their stalls.

We were given roasted apples and hot mince pies, in our nostrils were spices like myrrh, and in our wooden box, as we headed back for the village, there were golden gifts for all.

From *Cider With Rosie*, by Laurie Lee

HOT SPICED CIDER

1 quart apple cider
1 2-inch cinnamon stick
1 nutmeg, whole
3 to 4 cloves
3 to 4 allspice
1/2 tsp orange peel, grated

Combine all ingredients in a medium-
sized saucepan and bring to a boil.

Turn heat to low and simmer 5 minutes.

Serve in mugs and decorate with a
cinnamon stick in each mug.

*The crew of Gemini VI sang "Jingle Bells" on December 15, 1965.
They accompanied themselves on harmonica and bells, thereby taking the ancient
tradition of caroling to, pardon the expression, new heights.*

*C*arols, which means "song of you," are a serenading custom of English origin from the Middle Ages when groups called "waits" would travel around from house to house singing ancient carols and spreading the holiday cheer.

Some caroling customs go back to the first century, when songs written in Latin were sung as part of nativity plays. St. Francis of Assisi was known to encourage others in Christmas season singing.

Schedule a night this year to let your voice ring out with the joy of Christmas.

Dave Davidson

A FRAGRANT PRAYER

LORD, I SING A NEW SONG OF GLORY AND PRAISE TODAY.
I COULD SING OF CHRISTMAS EACH MONTH OF THE YEAR.
YOUR LOVE MOVES MY HEART, NO MATTER THE SEASON.
YOUR SON'S BIRTH IS A JOY TO ME EVERY MOMENT,
A CONSTANT REASON TO SING FROM THE HEART.

ANTICIPATION AND SURPRISE
ARE SEEN THROUGH A CHILD'S EYES.

ANTICIPATION

THE VIRGIN WILL BE WITH CHILD AND WILL GIVE
BIRTH TO A SON, AND THEY WILL CALL HIM IMMANUEL —
WHICH MEANS, "GOD WITH US."
MATTHEW 1:23

CELEBRATION HOPE RELATIONSHIPS INVITATION SHARING TRADITION MUSIC ANTICIPATION SAVIOUR
SECRETS FOR A SEASON OF C. H. R. I. S. T. M. A. S. SPIRIT

The Fragrance of Christmas

A child's heart of anticipation as he or she looks forward to Christmas is an inspiration to us all. Children seem to easily envision the future and are especially overjoyed by the prospect of surprises ahead. Advent is a season of readiness that helps us focus on our faith and prepare our hearts, minds, and souls for the miracle of Christmas.

The joy we see in a child anticipating the blessings of Christmas is the same recipe for hope God gives to each of us today. As long as we can look ahead and fix our eyes on Jesus, we will always have the hope of Christmas.

A JOURNEY TOWARD THE STABLE

HOW WILL THIS BE, MARY ASKED THE ANGEL,
SINCE I AM A VIRGIN? THE ANGEL ANSWERED.
THE HOLY SPIRIT WILL COME TO YOU.
Luke 12:34-35

It's beginning to look a lot like Christmas. Soon the bells will start. And the thing that will make them ring, is the carol that you sing, right within your heart."

There's so much to discover together . . . window shopping, card creating, popcorn opping, tree decorating, carol singing, snow man making, light stringing, cookie aking . . . sentiments flourish in this season of anticipation.

The weather begins its frosty foreshadowing, shoppers start like there is no stopping, nd on the radio we hear the music of a new holiday season.

Advent begins the fourth Sunday before Christmas and is a time to make ready for the oming of Christ. Sarah Hornsby describes this time of joyous anticipation.

> Advent is a time of wonder, of beginnings, of preparation. Advent is a wreath of pungent evergreens with candles glowing, reflecting on familiar faces, bringing a holy light to the ordinary.

Each year we are challenged to slow down and appreciate the spirit and the fragrance of the season. Consider this reflection by singer-songwriter Michael Card,

> Like so many other people, Susan and I forgot that Christmas is a season and not merely a day. We counted the shopping days, but overlooked the calendar of the early church. As soon as we began to celebrate the season of Advent, December became a journey, a journey toward the day of Christmas . . . a journey toward a stable and an impossible birth.

> This December we will depart from the busyness of the world and proceed, by God's grace, toward a quiet, simple, lowly place: the stable where the King of the universe will be born once again into our heart.

I WILL HONOR CHRISTMAS
IN MY HEART
AND TRY TO KEEP IT
ALL THE YEAR.
Ebenezer Scrooge

MEDITATION ON CHRISTMAS EVE

Night has fallen; the clear, bright stars are sparkling in the cold air; noisy, strident voices rise to my ear from the city, voices of the revelers of this world who celebrate with merrymaking the poverty of their Saviour. Around me . . . my companions are asleep, and I am still wakeful, thinking of the mystery of Bethlehem. Come, come, Jesus, I await You.

Mary and Joseph, knowing the hour is near, are turned away by the townsfolk and go out into the fields to look for a shelter. I am a poor shepherd; I have only a wretched stable, a small manger, some wisps of straw. I offer all these to You, be pleased to come into my poor hovel.

I offer You my heart; my soul is poor and bare of virtues . . . this little is all I have. I am touched by Your poverty, I am moved to tears, but I have nothing better to offer You, Jesus, honor my soul with Your presence, adorn it with Your graces . . . Jesus, I am here waiting for Your coming. Wicked men have driven You out, and the wind is like ice. I am a poor man, but I will warm You as well as I can. At least be pleased that I wish to welcome You warmly, to love You and sacrifice myself for You.

Written on Christmas Eve, 1902, by Angelo Giuseppe Roncalli, who later became Pope John XXIII.

CHRISTMAS WAS COMING

*A*s evening drew on, hearts beat fast with anticipation, hands were full of ready gifts. There were the tremulously expectant words of the church service, the night was past and the morning was come, the gifts were given and received. Joy and peace made a flapping of wings in each heart, there was a great burst of carols, the peace of the world had dawned, strife had passed away, every hand was linked in hand, every heart was singing.

From *The Rainbow* by D. H. Lawrence, 1885-1930

Christmas . . . meant great smells
from the kitchen — homemade bread
and cranberries bubbling on the stove,
pumpkin pies, and turkey.
Gloria Gaither

Standing at the window, sleepy children in slippers gaze into
the night sky searching for Christmas stars and red noses on reindeer.
Anticipation battles each yawn as they deny tired eyes. Soon dawn will fall
upon children full of hope and excitement for another Christmas morning.
                        Becca Lynn

CHRISTMAS EVE EXPECTATIONS

On Christmas Eve . . . I would stay awake all the moonlit, snow-lit night to hear the roof-alighting reindeer and see the hollied boot descent through soot. But soon the sand of the snow drifted into my eyes, and, though I stared towards the fireplace and around the flickering room where the black sack-like stocking hung, I was asleep before the chimney trembled and the room was red and white with Christmas.

From *A Prospect of the Sea* by Dylan Thomas

IT IS GOOD TO BE CHILDREN SOMETIMES, AND NEVER BETTER THAN AT CHRISTMAS, WHEN IT'S MIGHTY FOUNDER WAS A CHILD HIMSELF.
                        Charles Dickens

A CHILD'S WONDER OF CHRISTMAS

Life holds no sweeter thing than this:

To teach a little child the tale most loved on earth

And watch the wonder deepen in his eyes

There while you tell him of the Christ Child's birth;

The while you tell him of shepherds and a song,

Of gentle drowsy beast and fragrant hay

On which that starlit night in Bethlehem

God's tiny Son and His young mother lay. . . .

Adelaide Love

A FRAGRANT PRAYER

YOU'VE GIVEN ME THE EYES OF A CHILD'S HEART TO
RECEIVE SALVATION. I'M THANKFUL FOR THE GIFT OF YOUR
SPIRIT THAT GUIDES ME TO UNDERSTAND YOUR TRUTH.
KEEP ME EVER RELYING ON YOU EACH DAY
JUST LIKE A NEWBORN CHILD.

THE SAVIOUR'S HUMBLE BIRTH
GIVES PEACE TO ALL ON EARTH.

SAVIOUR

TODAY IN THE TOWN OF DAVID A SAVIOR HAS
BEEN BORN TO YOU; HE IS CHRIST THE LORD.
LUKE 2:11

CELEBRATION HOPE RELATIONSHIPS INVITATION SHARING TRADITION MUSIC ANTICIPATION SAVIOUR
SECRETS FOR A SEASON OF C. H. R. I. S. T. M. A. S. SPIRIT

The Fragrance of Christmas

The Christmas story in Luke, chapter 2 of the Bible,
lays the foundation for God's eternal plan for earth.
First, Christ was to be born in lowly form, yet fully divine.
Later, He would humble himself even unto death on a cross.
His mission was clear. He came to comfort the weary, to free
the imprisoned, and to save the lost.

God gave us His gift of grace against a backdrop of stars
shining, shepherds worshiping, and angels singing.
Let us remember, too, that He also gave us
the Saviour of the world.

THE TRUE CHRISTMAS SPIRIT

AND HE WILL BE CALLED WONDERFUL
COUNSELOR, MIGHTY GOD, EVERLASTING
FATHER, PRINCE OF PEACE.
Isaiah 9:6

Martin Luther witnessed the beauty of a German evergreen forest against a starlit sky. In awe of God's creation, he cut a tree and lit it with candles at home to celebrate the Saviour's birth on Christmas Eve.

Another traditional plant, with its brilliant colors during the holiday season, points us toward the greatest gift of Christmas.

Legend has it that the flowers of the plant were so tiny, they went unnoticed until the day Christ was crucified. As more of His blood fell, the leaves became permanently stained, transforming the bush into a beautiful new creation. It was discovered when the conditions were right it easily took root; just as Christ does in our heart.

When broken, the plant bled, not red but white, representing the purity of Christ's sacrifice. The flower and its surrounding leaves fade away, although they revive when the darkness of the night lengthens. This commemorates the dark day Christ died. Its color bursts forth in brightness, as Christ burst forth from the tomb.

The legend of the poinsettia points us to the cross and empty tomb of Jesus, representing the gift of new life to believers. The full fragrance of Christmas is captured only when we ask Him to be our personal Saviour.

The true Christmas spirit, is the Holy Spirit (Acts 15:8) who invites everyone at Christmas on God's behalf . . . to accept the ultimate gift of heaven.

THE VERY PURPOSE OF CHRIST'S COMING INTO
THE WORLD WAS THAT HE MIGHT OFFER UP HIS LIFE
AS A SACRIFICE FOR THE SINS OF MEN. HE CAME
TO DIE. THIS IS THE HEART OF CHRISTMAS.
Billy Graham

JESUS IS THE BEST GIFT

*T*he best gift you can give a child is Jesus Christ. If you want to do something good for the children in your life, if you want to give them the gift that keeps on giving, introduce them to Jesus Christ.

Get them completely involved in His church. Show them how important your faith is to you. Give them the real gift of Christmas, the gift of the Christ child. Help them discover the power of the Christian faith.

James W. Moore

WERE EARTH A THOUSAND TIMES AS FAIR,

BESET WITH GOLD AND JEWELS RARE,

SHE YET WERE FAR TOO POOR TO BE,

A NARROW CRADLE, LORD, FOR THEE.

Martin Luther

THANKS BE TO GOD FOR HIS INDESCRIBABLE GIFT!
2 CORINTHIANS 9:15

The Lord's Prayer at Christmas

The story has been published of a little girl caught in the pre-Christmas swirl of activity, all of which seemed to be coming to a head on Christmas Eve.

The little girl herself, trying to help, found that she was always under-foot, and sometimes adult kindness to her wore thin.

Finally, near tears herself, she was hustled off to bed. There kneeling to pray the Lord's Prayer before tumbling in, her mind and tongue betrayed her and she prayed, "Forgive us our Christmases as we forgive those who Christmas against us."

Too often we leave out the Christ of Christmas. Too often He is crowded out of our busy lives. Remember, the best gift won't be found in a box but in a person.

Anonymous

The greatest and most momentous fact which the history of the world records is the fact of Christ's birth.

Charles H. Spurgeon

Christmas Reminds Us . . .

. . . THAT WE NEED A SAVIOUR

Deep down inside — we all relate to Ebenezer Scrooge.
We all need help. We all need to be converted from
selfishness to love. We all need a Saviour.

. . . THAT WE NEED A SAVIOUR

This is indeed the good news of Christmas:
"Unto us a child is born, unto us a Saviour is given." No matter in
what circumstances we find ourselves, we can count on that.

. . . THAT WE NEED A SAVIOUR

Every time we show love for another person,
we are living in the spirit of Christ, we are sharing the
Saviour, we are keeping alive the power of Christmas.

James W. Moore, Christmas Gifts That Always Fit

MARY DID YOU KNOW

Mary did you know that your baby boy
will give sight to a blind man?
Mary did you know that your baby boy
will calm the storm with his hand?
Did you know that your baby boy
has walked where angels trod?
And when you kiss your little baby,
you've kissed the face of God.

Mark Lowry

A FRAGRANT PRAYER
FATHER, YOU'VE GIVEN ME THE OPPORTUNITY
TO KNOW JESUS, THE SAVIOUR OF MY SINS. I OPEN
MY HEART TO RECEIVE CHRIST TODAY. THANK YOU FOR
YOUR UNFAILING LOVE, UNDESERVED GRACE, UNENDING
MERCY, AND UNSURPASSED PEACE IN MY LIFE.

A CHRISTMAS PRAYER

Grant us the true Christmas spirit, Lord.
The generosity of heart, the self-forgetfulness, the
love which caused You to wrap yourself in the garments
of our humanity and live among us for a time.

Grant us the true Christmas spirit, Lord.
The genuine joy of authentic celebration — angels singing,
shepherds stumbling through the dark in search of the Savior,
Elizabeth's song, Simeon's prophecy, Anna's exclamation of praise!

Grant us the true Christmas spirit, Lord.
Hymns of faith sung from the heart, true worship,
candlelight communion, prayer more real than words. The simple
pleasure of family and friends, the excitement of children, adult
conversation laced with memories, childhood remembered and
relived for a day. Grant us the true Christmas spirit, Lord.

Richard Exley, *A Touch of Christmas*

For more of *The Fragrance of Christmas*
visit the authors' site on the web at,
ChristmasSpirit.com

Dan & Dave Davidson have written over a
dozen books using motivation, hope, humor, and
inspiration to encourage readers to reflect on their
own lives. They have shared the literary pen name of
Cyrano De Words-u-lac in several of their writing
projects. The brothers have formed the creative team,
ThinkWOW.com, with other writers and graphic artists. Special thanks to Becca Lynn and
Tim Moser for their contributions to *The Fragrance of Christmas*.

If you would like to make a submission for a future book or would like information
on speaking workshops, contact Dan & Dave Davidson at ThinkWOW.com / P.O. Box 1416 /
Salem, VA 24153 / email: davidson@ThinkWOW.com

Other New Leaf Press titles by Dan & Dave Davidson

A Cup Of Devotion With God (1998) — www.DailyDevotion.com